Brian Shepherd worked in the mental health service for much of his life. This book of poems describes a difficult time while working in a day-hospital, trying to achieve a work/life balance during various crises with both patients and management.

Brian is now retired and spends his time with family and friends. He is active in various campaigns such as global warming.

This book is dedicated to the patients and staff who were with me in these turbulent years.

Brian Shepherd

THE BAREFOOT THERAPIST

AUSTIN MACAULEY PUBLISHERS™

LONDON • CAMBRIDGE • NEW YORK • SHARJAH

A CIP catalogue record for this title is available from the British Library.

ISBN 9781035805624 (Paperback)
ISBN 9781035805631 (ePub e-book)

www.austinmacauley.com

First Published 2023
Austin Macauley Publishers Ltd®
1 Canada Square
Canary Wharf
London
E14 5AA

My thanks to:
Ruth Mawby
Bea Jay
Evie Fairclough
For their illustrations

Table of Contents

Foreword

In my retirement, I was looking through old papers and I came across the last copy of this book. Leafing through it brought back lots of memories and made me realise that a lot of the issues described in the poems were still taking place today, 40 years later.

The struggles of people at the bottom, the economic crisis, different approaches and treatments for people with mental health difficulties, the silent power of bureaucracy, maintaining a work/life balance, staff shortages in the caring professions and so on.

While a lot of these issues are still causative factors in today's mental health crisis, we have in addition other factors such as global warming and its threat to human survival, neo liberalism and global inequalities, a worldwide refugee disaster and the war in Europe.

I remembered also, how the poems had struck a chord with many in the therapeutic profession when the book was first published, and after discussing with colleagues whether there was any merit in having the poems republished, I concluded that they might strike a chord with a new generation facing so many similar issues.

Brian Shepherd 2023.

Introduction

The poems describe the attempt to remain sane while balancing the demands of working professionally, being a shop steward, looking after children and maintaining relationships with lovers and friends.

The poems are centred in the work place – a day-hospital in the grounds of a large mental hospital. They were written during a long and bitter struggle (The Ward Battle) over how the day hospital should be run.

The traditionalists, headed by the charge nurse, believed that the day hospital should be run no differently from any other ward in the hospital. The aim was to keep patients busy and the ward neat and tidy. It was based on a medical model of treatment and a political system of control from the top.

The medical model saw psychiatric illness as being similar to physical illnesses such as flu. The mental problem arose from some malfunction of the body which could be put right by the doctor's intervention. This would normally take the form of drugs, such as tranquillisers, given either as pills or injections, or, if they did not work, a course of ECT. The job of the nursing staff was to make sure the patient was clean, slept, ate his or her meals and did something useful during the day.

The political system which went with the medical model was both hierarchical and bureaucratic. Power was vested at the top in the psychiatrist who laid down the medical treatment. He or she then left the day to day administration in the hands of his or her deputy, the charge nurse. The charge nurse was only expected to keep his or her charges fed, clean and busy. The easiest way to make sure this happened was to set up a tight bureaucratic system which set times for different tasks and where everyone was in an allotted place for the appropriate period of the day.

Within this system junior staff had little capacity to initiate change. In fact, any who tried were immediately seen as being trouble-makers – trying to upset the smooth-running system. Order and accountability were what counted and ever more so as the public expenditure cuts began to bite.

The alternative model which most of the staff believed in (see the poem: How the Day Hospital Works) saw the aim of the unit as being to give patients control of their lives. The political system that underpinned this approach was a democratic one.

As regards treatment, while it was accepted that on occasions medication helped to stabilise patients, the main approach was to work with people through their problems by individual and group therapy. Mental illness was not seen as a physical problem but as arising from difficulties experienced by people in coping with the world. The three most common problems were: how families had treated children; women exploited by men, and people suffering from social and economic disadvantages. In order to tackle these problems, people needed both practical social skills and an understanding of themselves. They also needed to take responsibility for their actions and their consequences.

The political system underpinning this approach was one based on democratic principles where patients were given a maximum say in how they spent their day and in how the day hospital ran. Salvation was not seen to lie purely in the hands of the psychiatrist. Understanding and knowledge were things shared between patients and staff and between patients themselves. If patients were to participate in and control their treatment, then there was a need for openness and flexibility and hence for the minimum of bureaucracy.

There was little basis for compromise between the two systems and hence 'The Ward Battle[1]. The psychiatrist who was new and a bit unsure of himself stayed largely above the struggle. The rest of the hospital management saw the dangers (shades of solidarity, tenants' power, workers' control etc.) and rallied to the support of the charge nurse.

While each of the poems is based on a real incident, they do not attempt to be an accurate portrayal. In addition, names and scenes have been altered to protect people.

Brian Shepherd
July 1983

How the Day Hospital Works

So how do we work
In this day hospital
You will be reading about?

As will become clear
We believe that
The thoughts and feelings that people have
Arise out of the situations
That they have been
And are at present in.
It therefore follows
That for change to occur
People need to act
To alter the situation.
For example by:
Moving from a hostel to a flat;
Finding a job;
Getting off with someone.
If there is no action
Then therapy becomes merely
A means whereby people
Are persuaded against their real self interest
To accept their oppression.

The ability to act
Requires people having basic social skills.
Therefore, we run groups for:
Literacy and numeracy;
Cooking and social skills;
Do it yourself and art therapy;
Current affairs and problems of living alone;
Psychodrama and women's health.
It also requires people
To be aware of themselves and others,

So we started by doing
Individual and group therapy.
But gradually we made it possible
For therapy to happen
With most people most of the time
Whatever they were doing.

Slowly people build up a view
Of themselves and the world
And of how it can be changed.
Then there is nothing for them
But to jump,
And for us to hope
That the safety net we erect
Will catch any fallers.
You cannot wait,
As psychiatrists and social workers seem to think,
Until people are completely sure of what they want.
Think of the last holiday you booked.
Didn't you have doubts

Until the plane actually took off.
In the waiting, before the action,
There are only possibilities and doubts.

You don't normally have to go back
To people's childhood roots.
There is sufficient cause for their behaviour
In the worlds that have been constructed for them.

The people most difficult to help
Are married women with kids.

There's no escape.
Nothingness isn't recognised
As a cause for running.
Where could they and the kids go.
Living on S.S. crammed into a single room,
Just isn't worth the leaving.
Most of her friends would think her barmy.
The women's movement
Hasn't made it yet into the high-rise flats.
There's no basis,
It has nothing to offer.
It won't pay the rent,
Look after the kids,
Get her a job.
"I can't oppress another woman
By getting her to do my housework."
All we can offer is a refuge,
A temporary haven,
Until he complains

That the house is looking dirty.

We hug people a lot
And encourage them to touch each other.
Before you get horrified
You must remember
That most of our members
Have lived lonely, institutionalised lives
Where no one has fancied them.
If no one likes them
And shows it by touching
How can you expect them
To like themselves.
And if you don't like yourself
Then there's nothing worth saving
And there's no energy for changing.
In fact the only time
Most of the people will have been touched
Is when someone in authority
Has wanted to force them
To do something:
Like being locked up:
Or given ECT;
Against their will.
They will have been prodded,
Poked, herded and held down
Until they have been punished
For turning the jailors into jailors.
You should talk to our patients
About hospital violence
They have witnessed and experienced.

A bit of Rampton lives on in every asylum.

It is important to be honest and open.
If nothing else
Our patients are sensitive to vibes.
In the world of the mentally ill
That is the only thing to trust.
In the real world
They always act.

You can see it sometimes with the volunteers
Snapping on their bright, cheery face
Thinking that's what's wanted.
But the patients know
And don't come back.

As staff it doesn't mean
You lay your troubles on the patients.
On the bad days we all have
You just don't pretend
That you're all there
And adjust what you take on accordingly.

Patients come from institutions,
From psychiatrists and social workers
Where things are always hidden from them.
They are always writing comments
That the patients never see.
One snatched her doctor's notes.
He called the police
Who charged her with stealing NHS property.

It was the story of her life.
No wonder the patients get worried.
The health workers label it paranoia.
And if the patients try to find out
What's in their biography
By asking different members of staff
They are accused of playing off the staff
Against each other.
As patients can only guess
How those in authority see them
The patients must adapt their behaviour for each
To fit in with what they suspect is wanted.
They record the patient as being manipulative.

Often, I lie on the floor in therapy.
It seems to me that patients
Are always asked to sit or lie down
So that they are smaller than the doctor
Who thereby protects himself from attack.
Anyhow how can you do therapy unless you are relaxed?

It is important that staff on occasions
Make themselves just a bit vulnerable.
I mean to be fair
We are always asking them to give us
Their life histories as hostages,
When their whole experience
Is those case notes
Become bargaining points for their future.
Should we not give them

Some details about ourselves,
Just a little bit of power

"We hug people a lot"

So if we should destroy their trust
They can hurt us just a little.
Would it not make us a bit more careful
When we gossip and betray confidences
Or simply don't care enough?

Surely staff have quite enough power
By having titles and a salary.
A bit of scruffiness doesn't do any harm,
Or anything,
Which enables patients to tease us.
It is more difficult
To take someone you can laugh at
Too seriously.
The nicest thing
Is when two of our patients
Fancy each other
And turn themselves on.

It makes us all a bit better.
Though we have to be careful
Not to rush in
With our analytical clippers
And chop off its head.

Simon

Simon turned off his hearing aid.
There was nothing to hear.
No one told him anything nice.
That he was important.

They just wanted to know
What he wanted to do.
Montgomery had once praised him for his drilling.
He had killed a few Germans.
His wife had run off with another man.
A woman had once asked him to paint two rooms.
He had rescued his sister when her nightdress caught fire.
She had died four days later all black and burnt.

They didn't want to be drilled or killed
Or saved from fires.
Nothing else much had ever happened.
So, when they spoke to him
He turned off his hearing aid.
He sat in the library and read books
And began to dream
Of when he would die.
He would donate his body to science.

In his death he would become known
As his organs lived on.
Then one day he found himself
Sitting dressed in his coat
Waiting for the angel of death,
And he was already cold
Just as the doctor had predicted.

They talked him out of it of course.
It was their job after all.
Sane people live on into nothingness.
Anyway, who remembers the heart donor.
It is always the surgeon who gets the credit.

"Sitting dressed in his coat"

'Enlightened Psychiatry'

Jill went off to the hospital again today.
It was time for her fortnightly shot of ECT.
She had had it regularly since she was 22.
She was now over 40.
She was beyond complaining,
The headache normally went in a few hours.
Anyway, what was the use?
If she allowed herself to get disturbed
They simply electrocuted her once a week instead,
On the premise no doubt
That the fewer brain cells she had
The fewer there were to malfunction.

It also meant of course
That she didn't have much brain left
To do anything else satisfactorily.
Sometimes when talking with her
She would get half a thought out
Or a part-expressed feeling would get lost
As if the cells necessary to make the connection
Had been burnt away.
Which was the case.
It made it difficult

To help her work through her problems.
When she was twenty, she had run away with a man
Who forced her to do things
That she found repulsive.
When she came back, in a disturbed state,
Two years later,
The enlightened psychiatrist
Told her parents that on no account
Must they talk to her about this episode in her life.
He proceeded to reinforce his advice
By blasting her brain
Every time the experience surfaced
To upset her.

Now when we try to help her,
To work through her bubbling memories
We find that they and her mind
Are too fragmented
For anything to hold together
Long enough for sense to be made.

We sprung her to a hostel
Where at least she is free
To have an occasional adventure.
But to be safe,
Before they finally released her
The psychiatrist had her sterilised.

Bruce

"Nasty, crusty old man,
Syphilitic, dogmatic,
Authoritarian, fascist,
How can I relate to you?"

Bruce in his own way loved Penny.
He ordered her around like a naval rating
When he had time left from ordering everyone else around.
He hated blacks, scruffs, and most people who had ever lived.
He knew he was right
And didn't need you to tell him otherwise.
He had served in the war,
Had worked hard in a plastics factory,
He had been betrayed by his wife.
He knew what was what,
And didn't need you to tell him otherwise.

He terrified me and the other staff.
We didn't always have the energy to take him on
Let alone establish a working relationship.

"He hated blacks, scruffs, and most people who had ever lived."

He was the only patient whom I wouldn't mind
If they zapped his brain.
In the end we decided to get rid of him,
Recommended that he go to the main hospital,
Decided his problem was a failure to maintain
His drug dosage.
It was easier than admitting we didn't know
What to do with fascists.
What do you do with a man who, in art therapy,
Draws Nazi symbols?
Report him to the Commission for Racial Equality?
Decide he's mad?

You couldn't reason with him,
Work therapeutically
And he poisoned the atmosphere for others

Whom we could love
Because we could control them,
They didn't have the protection of dogmatism.
They were just poor, harmless people
Dying for a touch of love and words of kindness,
Which was so gratifying to give.
And that's how we survived against all the odds
To live to give another day.

Notes on Working

Sometimes when I get home
I just fall asleep,
Too tired to talk to her,
Too tired to screw,
And even the knob
Of the mindless television
Is too far away.

She said, "Take the day off.
I want you to look after me.
I've got as much right
To your time as they have."

How do I explain I can't.
The patients don't stop coming.
If I stay away
It's the other staff who suffer,
Coping with my load.

If they become pissed off
The bitterness replaces the love
And without the love who can heal?
Then we become closed and divided

And without openness there is no trust.
Without trust who will talk?
Or let their feelings go?
Who can then grow?

It takes time for them and us both
To learn that we don't
Have to exercise our power
Remain the psychiatric jailors;
That some of us some of the time,
Will betray our employers
And fight alongside.
Otherwise
What's the point of being at work?

When there's a day's holiday
I'm too tired to enjoy it.
My head aches.
All I do is sleep.

Sometimes,
We the staff
Are treated more childlike
Then the patients.
They are told to stand on their own feet,
To make their own decisions.
We have to beg for permission
To change the way we work,
To be allowed to work collectively.
No wonder we are rebellious,
That hospital wards function like prison.

There are meetings most nights.
Left caucuses, rank and file gatherings,
Shop steward's committee, cuts group.
And then at work, amidst therapy,
The phone rings and it is a member's grievance,
A confrontation with management,
A struggle to be won or lost.

Sometimes the mind won't switch, click on.
The union, meeting seems unreal
Beside the individual's pain.
Other times I want to hide,
It all becomes too much,
Occasionally, with others,
I feel strong.
Then, wherever it is
They can be taken on.

The patients ask for trust, care affection and love.
All finite things
That need watering to survive.
Which is why the staff
Need first to love each other.
For criticism can only be taken
Within a deep bed of affection.

Leave me alone!
I've got my kids to worry about.
I'm sorry I'm irritable,
But Jane was upset this morning,
She's expecting her first period,

You want me to stay late and talk of solidarity.
Who is going to get my kids their tea?

Except for the May Day parade
Union meetings are drab childless affairs,
Composed of the unmarried, the once married,
And the unhappily married with widowed spouse.
The creche is non-existent,
The babysitting service unheard of.
It's a funny kind of socialism
Listening to the spokespeople of the different factions
Arguing the merits of their case,
Fighting for positions.

I work best the nights I sleep alone,
Don't bother to use the phone,
Control my commitments.

Sometimes I just want to fuck all night,
Or there's a crisis to be talked through,
Or we just snap and sleep stays away.
but next day they're all there,
Difficult and disturbed as normal.
All *I* can do is coast.

And hope that my friends
Will pick up the slack,
Cope with the crises.
The alternative is to wish
The difficult ones would go away,
Leaving the institutionalised

Who can only see and feel the grey
But then what would be the point?
It is as they say,
The integration of the personal
That will win the day.

If the staffing ratios were okay,
If we got paid a decent wage,
If the holidays reflected the emotional toil,
If, if, if, if,
If we were not paid to be warders,
If women were free,
If the revolution had come,
Then it would not be so hard,
Given there are only 24 hours a day,
To achieve the balance
Between work, friends and children,
Lovers, political activity,
Being alone, surviving.

Lyn

(i) The First Time

She sat crying – quietly
As she told me
Of the scissors, razor blades and darts
That she kept swallowing.

She told me her story.
Bear with me, reader.
By now you might be thinking,
No, not another tear-jerking tale.
We all have problems.
It can't be that which drives them mad.

She was it turned out
Rejected at birth by her mother
Who preferred boys.
Already at the age of 7
She had been sent
To a boarding school
For backward children
She wasn't subnormal
Just difficult to handle.
It's always the weakest

Who get defined as the problem,
Who are the guilty ones?
Never the mother, never the husband.
Not surprising therefore
That when she was raped
By her father when she was 16
That her mother blamed her
And she blamed herself.
That was when she started swallowing things,
To punish herself
For being so wicked
And to procure the abortion
Which would stop her once again
Giving birth to such monster parents.

By a miracle
She found herself a boy friend
Who loved her and held her
But didn't want to screw.
He proposed, she accepted.
But lightening always dogs
The feet of the oppressed.
Two weeks before the date
He was killed in a car crash.

She went on the road then,
Sleeping rough in the summer,
Going into a mental hospital for the winter.
She's institutionalised they say,
Doesn't want to leave hospital.
"Of course, I am," she said,

"where else do I feel safe?"

Oh reader, what do we do to each other every day
That the only place she wants to be
Is where you and I can't find her.
Might it really be.
That we are such monsters after all,
That how we talk and touch each other
Is more than most of us can cope with.

(ii) The Next Time

I watched a man dying.
It was quite a pleasant day
As he lay there in the grass
Oblivious to the people walking blindly past.

I am going to shut my eyes to you, Lyn
Next time you threaten me again
By swallowing darts, pins, needles,
Glass and other things
For which you hope to punish us
For not caring enough.

We rushed to your side,
Gazed wondrously at your X-rays,
Marvelled at yet another operation scar,
Gasped at how close you came to death.

When I returned from holiday
You had just come out of hospital
Having swallowed many things
Because you had been left alone
And then hassled
By a male's wandering hand.

You had only to remonstrate with him.
What's so difficult about talking
That you find it easier to cut your insides apart?
Are you so scared of being rejected
That you have to bleed
To bind us to you?
I saw you playing with the scissors,
Take the pins and Chris told me about the dart.
I freaked a bit;
Allowed you to get to me.
I felt:
Guilty about having gone off for a week;
Jealous of the relations you had built up with other
Members of staff;
Scared of losing my witch doctor's powers
If you could flaunt me.
So I tried too hard
To get through to you
Believing if you could feel the concern
You would stay your hand.
It nearly worked.
Then my confused emotions helped to make you doubt
And you slipped away to the loo.
When you came back
With a smug smile on your face
1 knew though you denied it,
What had happened.

You got your ride
In the ambulance
All the way to the main hospital

Where hundreds of us
Fought for you.

It can't go on my love.
Next time,
And there will be a next time, won't there?
We'll let you get on with it.
I was going to say
We can't take responsibility for your life,
But it doesn't ring true.
It's…
That you can't make us into warders
To create a prison cell
In which you exist in a strait jacket
Unable to swallow anything
But the strained baby food
We, your loving parents, provide
Through the tube we stuff down your throat.
You want the loving control
Of the family you never had
And for which most of us
Lives only in the pages
Of women's magazines
And political party programs

You're at a crossroads.
We won't buy your blood any longer,
And the doctors have said
They won't open you up any more.
You could learn to trust.
But that would mean

Turning your back on your experiences of life.
So first, instead of punishing yourself
You must learn to hate 'them'…
Men! Social Workers! The system!
Whoever they may be for you.
By joining with others
To wreak your revenge.
You will become called comrade
And in the new sisterhood
Built upon struggle
Feel free at last to trust.

But to get from S to B
When you are still entranced
With the glitter of silver.
Even those of us
Who have learnt from betrayal
Don't find the path easy.

All I know is that
Next time you will die.

In the park
The corpse has rolled over.
It's nothing but a drunk
Sleeping it off.

I suppose Lyn
That it's just that the demon drink
Is a more acceptable way
To do it

And luckily, I don't know his name
And he doesn't know mine.

Notes on Management

Day hospital staff working in isolation.
In their separate places,
Nervously prowling among their patients,
Dreading the periodic visit
Of the management bullies,
Out to stop anything
Which threatens to trample trouble
Across their field of responsibility.

They always come to talk to him (the charge nurse)
We, the other workers don't exist.
There is a procedure.
We talk to him.
He talks to them.
They forget about it.

He said, "I'm on your side."
We snorted – you, the management,
Who never talk to us,
Pretend we don't exist,
Whom we have to threaten
With industrial action
To get any satisfaction.

You! On our side?

This is the way hierarchies work.
The top management tells
the middle management who tell
the lower management who tells
Us, the workers, what to do.
But the theory goes wrong here,
Because they don't know what we do.
Or, more importantly,
How we do it.

They can only ask about what they understand:
Have you filled in your forms correctly?
Have you overspent your budget?
Make sure there are no complaints.
Do your numbers meet the quota?
Has there been my damage to our property?
And so on and so on.

The office gets filled with forms
And the sound of typewriters and calculators
Sending the replies upwards.
In the ward,
The therapeutic community
Chugs along in fits and starts
Running on its own emotional lifeblood.

The thing about talking to management
Is that it is very boring.
They have nothing to say but pleasantries.

However, they know that I know,
That being pleasant
Is the last thing I want to be
Or they know how to be.

How can you be honest
With people who believe
In a public morality
Derived from the popular press,
Who think that occasional lovers
Are a disease called nymphomania.
That separated people
Suffer from the mark of Cain;
That children brought up by single parents
Are children at risk.

So we can't tell them
Who we really are.
The patients know.
They're like us,
Ordinary people, torn apart,

"Sit behind a desk, exuding authority"

badly stitched together
Occasionally coming apart at the seams.

If you wear a tie and a suit,
Printed dress and a hat,
Sit behind a desk,
Exuding authority,
Under a sign
Saying doctor or manager,
You cannot expect people to see you,
Other than as a
Reincarnated John Wayne
Killing the gooks,
The patients.

The trouble with the union,
According to the management
Is that it won't accept
That they know best.
Telling workers they're underpaid,
Encouraging them to file grievances,
To make demands.
God forbid – if it's not stamped on
Then it might be – workers control!
And then even worse.

The workers could give control to the patients,
The clients, the handicapped,
The elderly, the disturbed,
The downcast, the insane,
The poor and the meek
Would inherit the earth.
Not in our life time they said,
That only happens when we're dead

Adam and Mary

I used to get angry
At Mary and Adam
For not saving
For their future;
I mean,
They had been engaged
For at least nine months;
Until they made me realise
That they had no future.

They just kept on;
Ignoring our advice,
Threats and case reviews;
Living at her hostel
And his mum's
Getting full board,
Spending their pocket money
On booze and bookies.
And the occasional joint
Falling in and out of each other.

They didn't see
Why they should move into a bedsitter

To show us they could survive
So we would get them a flat
Where they would live on social security
Struggling to pay their
Rent, rates, food, and heating bills,
Filling their time with
Cooking, washing, cleaning
Shopping and budgeting
And having to put up with each other
24 hours a day,
7 days a week,
52 weeks a year.

Most of us
Can't manage that,
Let alone people who come to us
Because they have problems relating.

Why should they grow up?
There's nothing much in it
According to most folks I talk to.

As always it's you and me and us
Who want them to change
To be like us
But they're okay
Drifting aimlessly
Occasionally enjoying themselves,
Waiting,
Until the boredom gets too much.

The Children's Hostel

Ann fell in love with Peter
And he with her.
One day he asked her to marry him.
She accepted and they went to bed.

The next morning the moral vultures pounced.
Eve had brought sin into the children's home.
Hounded, persecuted, she retreated
Crying: I'm frightened, and said no more.

"Mad," they cried, "she's mad, she's guilty
Lock her up, lock her up."
The GP said she's disturbed.
The social worker whipped her to the shrink
Who said, welcome, you need some rest
We, the authorities know what's best.

The hostel shut their eyes
Then their front door,
When Ann wanted to come back.
Ann said, "I want to be back with Peter."
The hospital said, "She's alright."
Peter said, "Help, I don't know what's going on."

The hostel said simply, "She's mad,
She's upset, she feels, she lives,
Quieten her down, you know,
The drugs, the ECT, the injections,
If she won't cooperate
You can always tie her down,
You're clever, you'll know what to do."

The psychiatrist sat in splendour
Amidst his admiring harem of juniors
And holding Ann up by his arrogance
Admonished her for being so quiet.

Ann came back home.
With a little support
(all she had needed)
She was soon not alone.
She and Peter sat holding hands
For that's all that kids do isn't it!
Planning their future, wedding dress and all
If we can arrange their escape
Past the wardens of the state.

Paul

Paul heard Ruth today.
Her voice spoke to him,
To his soul, his unwin
And he was too shy
To talk to her;
So he reinvented her
With his psychic powers
Turned her into a 'fact',
Into his reality.
There she brought peace to
And ordered his mind,
Drove out the devil
Who was ready to bite off his head.

Ann

Exhausted I wrote a poem about Ann
Who they locked away as a scarlet woman
For the sin of sleeping with a man
In the same bed, in a hostel
Where people are children
Who must not grow up.

The mad must be dispossessed.
Not because of who they are
But because of what they have done
Or have done to them.
If we certify the individual
Then it's not us, it's them.
It's not our responsibility,
The way we live our lives.
If Ann were not bad and mad
Then we might have to face the fact
That sex can be enjoyable.
But if only the mad have fun
We must preserve our sanity
However grim the struggle.

The Ward Battle

(This is a severely edited account of a 2-year conflict in between the charge nurse backed by different managers and myself as deputy and the staff team on the underlying philosophy of how the ward should be run. The poem in the original publication ran to over 30 sections.)

We tried to explain to the charge nurse
What a therapeutic centre was
How his day hospital actually ran.

How over the months
We had all become sensitised
To each other's emotional vibes.
How in the trust that has built up
We could all, patients and staff,
Explore, and work out in detail,
The relationships that existed
Inside and between each of us.

Because he always sat in his office
He wasn't part of this emotional life.
He still saw a regime
Where structure should dominate
(Who should be in what group)
Where the content of the program

(cooking, literacy, art, crafts etc.)
Was all important,

How do we explain to you
That people are not problems
To be solved, categorised,
And tucked away.
That a person in difficulty
Doesn't have to be a threat to your defences,
How in openness and trust
You can confront and change.
You can act
Reluctantly
How you think we would like you to be.
But it is only an act.
There is no change of heart.
To put it simply – You just don't love people.

Once you have decided
That difficulties are solved
By being locked away in the unconscious
You have lost part of yourself
And used up a lot of energy
Making sure the doors are memory tight,
More importantly,
There's a part of you that others can't find
And can't find that part in themselves.
It's just these parts
Which bind and blind people to each other.
"You're the deputy,"
The nursing officer said.

"Why don't you give more support to your charge nurse."

"Look," I said,
"I could only act as a go between
When there was general agreement
Where the whole place was going.
But it changed, the charge nurse didn't."
The gap became too big to be bridged,

We had reached the limit.
The charge nurse had at least glimpsed
The sea of emotions we worked in
But feared his defence would be breached
If he jumped in.
But if the rest of us
Were not to tire and drown
He had to be prepared to at least paddle.

But there was a problem.
If we called a truce
How was the deal to be enforced?

I awoke at quarter to three this morning.
There was no energy left
To sleep or dream anymore.

It's one of the signs
That they've won.

The compromise couldn't be stable
Because if there was no change

Then neither us nor the patients could grow.

The charge nurse who had only accepted
The compromise
Because he had to,
Fought a rear-guard action against us
Slowing everything down
By hiding in his office
Where he whiled away his time
Constructing pyramids of red tape.

I read for an hour
And woke her up.
I turned away
It was all I could manage.
I was empty inside.

Then the nursing officer appeared,
The charge nurse had fled,
The nursing officer had no option but to
Listen to us.
So we told him the way it was

The unbridgeable gap between him and the rest
Of us.
In the nicest possible way of course,
We are, after all, the most reasonable of
Caring people.

Oh baby, I am going to buy you the universe
This weekend,
For,
We have killed the fucking bastards.

Yesterday we killed them.
The next day they tried to kill us,
The big one came down
With the nursing officer.

The big one said:
We must uphold the system,
Support the officer in charge, otherwise,
He wasn't bright enough to find the words,
But what he meant was,
Workers would rule,
Patients take control of their lives,
Social control would disappear,
Hierarchies collapse,
Bureaucracies burst,
The revolution would have arrived,
Anarchy would reign.
So the big one did his macho number,
Threatened we would all be fired

If we didn't toe the line.
But we were unmoved.

The big one then called me in
And tried to say it was all my fault,
That as deputy, I had not built the bridge,
That I should go
And the rest could then be crushed.
I was unmoved.

Yesterday we had nine people
In some sort of crisis.
There were three of us to deal with them
And keep the 30 others occupied.
The charge nurse played with his books in the morning
And went for a drive in the afternoon.
Today we were told management will speak to each other
And then come down and deliver to us their commandments,
But they'll only contain words
As they sit back and wait
For the charge nurse to leave
In his own good time.

But in the waiting
We feel our death.

I sit alone in the pub.
My friend lies in my bed.
I can only think of war, but
She wants peace in my head.

I become the enemy.
I lose you.
I am afraid.

The bastard, the nursing officer
Has broken his word.
Having said he wasn't prepared to wait.
We sit…
While the charge nurse applies unsuccessfully
For job after job.

We work
Our personal life collapses.

We might include the tale
Of the social worker
Who came to an emergency case review
Who proceeded
With the charge nurses' encouragement
To try and sell us all jewellery.
Though to be fair to the social worker,
Given this is a materialistic society,
It is far more profitable
To live off the poor
Then to help them.

Over gin and tonics and
Halves of lager
The nursing officer told me
That he was my friend
But that I should be warned

That if I threatened to take action
Then this would confirm
The malicious rumours
And I would not get the charge nurse's job.

Keeping a tight hold on myself.
You are after all
Not allowed to shake nursing officers
And especially not in the middle of a crowded pub,
I said there was a limit.
I was already exploited.
I was not prepared to be bullied also.

I felt good.
Having stood up for what I believed
And not sold anyone out.
For as I had pointed out to him
If I had listened to his advice
There wouldn't be
Any point
In making me a charge nurse.

I awoke, sweaty and anxious,
Dreaming about the negotiations
I had been having
In and out of forests
At desks on building sites
And offices in spatial mansions,
With the big one's big one.

The dream could also have been about Mary.

Likely this weekend to take all her remaining pills
In a kamikaze Molotov cocktail,
And my anxiety
That I had done all I could to help her.
Perhaps if I had persuaded more
She would have seen the consultant again
And found the lump was merely a cyst
That could be easily and painlessly removed.
No, rather I knew
That she trusted me
And wanted my energy
To help her struggle through,
Which, in practice meant
That I would see her night and day
Because
If I was always on call
A reservoir to draw upon
Then the struggle might just be bearable.

But instead
As she knew
I was setting off
For a mucky weekend
Out of contact
While she lay tossing in pain
Counting relentlessly the
Millions off sheep and stars
That inhabited her nights
Having already told me
That she was going to be alone
Was going to lock the front door

And…

What Mary?
A long pause.
I don't know

I am at the other side of midnight
In the dungeons of my mind.
I go to sleep with the light on
Listening to the music
Until that too falls into the void
And I awake.

We have reached the end.

An interlude – the staff meeting
The Angel of Death waits in the wings
We lie in our death
Mother hovers
Exhorting her children
To hit out at the fathers
Who threaten her.

The law has abandoned us.
We feel defenceless, betrayed,
Unwilling to let the children suffer.
The judges say you must wait for the due process of the law.
We cannot.
We have reached the end.
The charge nurse has entered a time warp
And acts as if the last 18 months

Haven't existed.

The inquiry has imprisoned
Our management support
In their bureaucratic cells.

Our anger and impotence
Turn us intro zombies
Who can no longer see, touch or speak meaningfully
To the freaked-out patients.

Since the second inquiry began
We have lost five back to the main hospital,
Five deaths
And the ward is beyond grieving,
There's something wrong
When you can't mourn the dead.

The deaths lie on my brain tonight.
The waste, the sheer fucking waste of these months.
I saw three of the corpses today,
Grinning inanely
Cabbages living on chemicals.

I killed you my Mary
When I took you in.
Left you among the others
Trying to climb out of windows,
Smoking rolled up bits of newspaper,
Threatening violence,
Mouthing nonsense.

And I left you there.
I had nothing anymore Mary.
I'm sorry.
I tried at least to find a place
Where they would treat your head and body together
But they told me
Heads were in a different catchment area
To wombs and breasts.
Sorry about that.

I feel hollow.
We're about to be crushed like vermin,
Sold out this time
By the labour party
What do you expect…
Who support the senior management
Who've decided to support
The charge nurse
And are at present
Gathering like vultures
Plotting how next week
They will descend en masse
To obliterate the community.
A blot of excellence
Dirtying their otherwise landscape of mediocrity
Which is after all
Bureaucratically speaking
So much more comfortable
And doesn't get in the way
Of the efficient compiling of reports of words which have no
meaning

Good God! They're only committee documents.
You mean we actually have workers
Who do this sort of thing?
Can't have that
Said the chairman
Don't know where it will end,
Support the hierarchy at all costs,
It's after all
What we are in the business of.

Down, down, down
Wanking in my bed
To induce the sleep
To block out the depression.
Work a bitter memory,
Therapy a dead word.

Yesterday the right-hand man
Protected by his bodyguards
Came to tell us officially
That charge nurses are infallible
And must always be obeyed.
We are not here to cure
Only to care, help and support them.

We are shattered and gone.
No energy left to pursue further grievances.
We'll leave them with their pyrrhic victory.
Not that they see it as such.
"Forty patients
Six staff,

All correct and present sir."
That's the spirit charge nurse.

I do not know
Freud, Jung, Lacan
In which galaxy
Your planets roam.

I come from a world
Where women, children and men
Are set on fire,
Beaten and humiliated.
Locked in cupboards and rooms,
Threatened and bullied
Bundled from home to hospital
And back again
By decree of the absent landlord
Of their soul.

It is a barren planet
Where there is no love,
No affirmation, no joy,
No purpose
Other than that of a chemical existence
And a brain jolted spasmodically
Into flickering existence
By switching on the electric current.

Today in confession
I learnt of children
Locked all day

In their bedroom
With nothing but their shit to play with.

Yesterday a social worker
Sat and told May
How they had moved her child
From a foster mother
Where the placement had broken down
(their fault they admitted)
Without telling her.

There was no lack of communication.
No missing language.
Life was survival
And the wasteland
Provided nothing
For anything to exist
Which might help people cope
With the tragedies yet to come.

In this world of benign cruelty
Our ward has become
Yet another planet
In which love is
Daily extinguished.
No wonder that tonight
I feel so much desolation
For the days yet to come
The pain to be experienced.

The charge nurse

So recently confirmed
In his position as first secretary
Of the ward committee
Has made his first ask
The production of a new timetable
To administer order and control
Among staff and patients.
This is after all
To be a well-run state.
As the left-handed lady herself said,
"You can't do anything
Until you know
They have clean underwear on each day."

According to the programme
I am to spend my time organising activities
Such as monopoly, scrabble and Lego
That way management will know
There is no longer any risk
Of my curing a patient
Something they have decided
Only psychiatrists are allowed to try.

The left-handed woman descended
to deliver a sermon
On a deputy's duty to his superiors.
If you could not honour
You should at least obey.

The left-handed woman continued:
You should impose your joint decisions

On the rest of the staff

And lay waste any remaining pockets of opposition.

She comforted us.

Don't worry that the ward lies in emotional ruin;

It's a small price to pay

In terms of the whole service

As you realise that when faced with your El Salvador

You, with our aid, stood firm at last,

Stopped the revolution

And saved our way of life.

Helen, Amy, Elizabeth and Miranda

"She tried it with John, the man from next door.
Made all his meals and washed down the floor.
Had two of his kids, made up her face,
Tried ever so hard to keep a neat place.
However too soon she also did find
That inside the house she was outside her mind.
That like all her friends to the doctor she went,
Two pills at breakfast, the health visitor sent."
So, once they take your kids away

And your husband is indifferent,
And no one sees your housework,
Or how you struggle to make ends meet,
And sex is no more than the spreading of legs,
And there's nothing but the daily dust,
The shopping and the kids getting on your nerves,
Then how do you escape other than by going mad?

But they, the men, don't let you.
They take you down to the doctors,
They hold you down while they stuff more pills
Down your throat.
And if you still don't wake up walking dead
They put an electric fire in your brain.
They turn you into an autonom,
Their very own robot
To service their needs.
"Wash...the...clothes
Clean...the house
Make...my ...dinner."
And if you're good
Once a week they'll take you out
Making sure that you're dressed up first,
Their very own baby doll
To show off and then ignore,
While they down their well-earned beers.
It's hard work, thirsty work, men's work,
Keeping a housewife,
Driving a woman mad.

All you want is that he will hold you.

Just hold you.
Let you let go.

Please, please just hold me,
Let me, let me be,
Let me relax.

Oh! No!
I don't want that fucking weapon
Inside me anymore.

– yanking at it –

Oh! No!

Please stop.
You're hurting.
You're hurting me.
Take your hands away from my throat.
Don't hit me again.
I'm sorry.
I'll be gentle.
Here, here, put it in,
There's a big boy,
Come to mommy.

There's nothing like being affirmed.
Being mentally ill
Is being negated.
There is nothing more depressing

Then not existing.

Oh! God! Johnny,
Go back to bed.
It's only six o'clock.
Quiet! You'll wake daddy.
Oh! I'm coming.
You're big enough to have a pee on your own.
Quiet!
What's happening?

God! Look what you've done you brat.
It's nothing.

You know I need my sleep,
Can't you even control the kids – Christ!

Quick Johnny back to bed.
Alright, alright, I'll make breakfast,
But quietly.
What's going on now?

Just getting the kid his breakfast.

You could at least offer to bring me a cup of tea.
Do I have to do everything around the house myself.

Well, here's the cornflakes.

I don't want cornflakes, I want sugar puffs.
We don't have any.

I want sugar puffs
If you don't give them to me, I'll scream.
Johnny!

"What's going on down there;
God woman how do you expect me to spend more
Time at home.
More money for this,
Why don't I do more with the kids,
You never stop nagging,
It gives me a pain in the arse
To be at home with you.
You can't even look after the kids.
And where's the cup of tea?
I'm the one who has to go out and earn the
Money.
You've got nothing to do all day."

"Came home one day, husband had gone,
Couldn't work out what she had done wrong.
The neighbours said it was all her fault
Clever young girls just didn't get caught.
Kids got too much, the state took them away,
Put them in care, she saw them Sunday.
They gave her a social worker all of her own
Who seduced her one day when they were alone."

How's life Joyce?
No use complaining.
What's your old man like?

I could tell you a few things about him
But I won't and I don't.
I'm not really sure why not.
I don't like the fucker.
But he's all I've got.
I failed first time around,
And with three kids in tow
I've got nowhere else to go.

The Union

Looking around the hall,
The last branch executive of the year,
Perhaps mine for some time.

If the charge nurse goes
And I'm offered his job,
Then I can't remain a steward.

The simplest explanation
Is that I'll be too busy.
True enough
But not enough.

Time to give others a go,
Gain experience,
The union should not become
A careerist battleground,
A gathering of elites.
True,
But still not enough.

I'll have become a manager,
Changed my base,

Become wealthier,
Committed to running the ward well.
I couldn't be trusted any longer
To always put the interests of my workers first.
My loyalties would be divided.
I need to balance my power,
Whether exercised or not,
By encouraging one of the other workers
To become the steward.

He paused
And heard the malicious whisper:
'Sell out'
Spreading,
Fingers pointing,
Voices denouncing,
Three billion unemployed,
Comrades dismissed, laid off,
Cuts hitting working conditions
And take-home pay.
Now is not the time
For activists to leave,
There are few enough already.

I say,
When challenged,
That socialism consists of many different struggles,
That the abuses of psychiatry in particular
And the welfare state in general
Need also to be confronted.
That I will be in a position to do this

And transform the social relations
Between some of the oppressed,
Their exploiters
And the middle women and men
Like myself.

Alternatively
This might all be a lot of flannel,
A self-justification
For being unable
To recognise my Trojan horse
My very own ward
With its trappings of
Status, control
And the luxury of being able to try out
(with the co-operation of others)
My ideas in practice.
How different
From an academic
His/her well paid ivory tower
Captive audiences and publications.

Fuck!
But if I'm proved wrong
Then I can always resign
And go back down the ladder to
Where one needs to struggle
Just to survive.
But remember
You will soon be 40.
Will it still be possible next time?

So round and round to the sound of the breaking glass
And look what happened to you Hazel O'Connor.
If you want
What they want you to want
Then you will only get success
On their terms.
And that's no victory at all.

It isn't easy down among the fragments.

The Group

Bill is going to kill Harold.
Most of the other patients
Will support him.
Harold is a thief and a vandal
Who doesn't own up to things.
People suspect
But can't prove.
Harold gloats
But hides in the library
Until he is sure
Bill has gone home.

Harold accused Bill
Of stealing some money
He only pretended he had lost
So as to get out of repaying Margaret
What he owed her.
Bill was angry.
Yet someone else
Was exploiting his kindness.
Those who have nothing
Can only eat each other.
Also everyone believes

That Harold broke the billiard cues,
Which he did
Because he failed to make it with Margaret
In the bathroom.
But so far the only witness
Will only testify privately.

Should we pressure him
To own up?
Is that just an easier option
Then coping with Bill's anger?
Or let everything take its own good course, knowing,
That the first time something can be proved
The group will suspend him for weeks
If someone doesn't thump him first.

'From the Cultural Revolution'

"I asked her family:
|Why didn't you take her to a doctor?
Her husband told me angrily
That he had and the doctor had said
She was incurable.
I learned from the husband
That the doctor came from my hospital.
When I returned, I looked through the files
And found that the doctor
Who had made the incorrect diagnosis
Was me."

I have resigned from the union.
I have lost my anger,
Become too close to management.
It is time to give the power
To the lowest workers,
To those who are most pissed upon
With the least rewards
And retreat to being an advisor.

My anger is directed to new targets.
Our ward is becoming a focal point

In our area
Because we treat the patients as people.
We ask those:
Social workers, nurses, wardens and psychiatrists;
Who still treat the people as patients
Why?
They feel threatened
With their defences
Professionalism, book knowledge and
The order of institutional life
Under attack.
So now our ward is under siege.

Only yesterday
I was reported
For not consulting (getting permission from,)
A warden (the father),
Before asking a patient (the daughter),
Whether she wanted a friend (the lover),
To be present at her case review.

When the charge nurse finally goes
Management will have to decide
Whether to promote me
In the full knowledge,
After the policy meetings,
Of the waves to come.

In the meantime
We are here
The barefoot psychotherapists

Mingling daily with the people
Learning from them
That the problems
Lie in us out here
And in how we organise society,
Though of course our books say
That the problems
Exist in them
And have nothing to do with you or me,
Except, of course,
To give us our livelihood.

"I returned to the countryside
And took up my work.
I did not so much cure the peasants.
In truth they cured me.
Of my ideological sickness."

Quotes are a paraphrase of pp. 273-4
Maria A. Macciocchi: Daily Life in
Revolutionary China, New York Monthly
Review,172.[1]

1

Mary

As I lie in, my bed at home
You reach me.
I wonder whether you are still alive.
Is tonight the night
It all gets too much?
Is that what you are trying to tell me?
Or am I just listening to my anxiety of the day
Reflecting on what encounters I could have handled better?
I will phone tomorrow
Hoping that:
The ever-present pain from the mastectomy,
The new lumps and the smell of death,
The throbbing thyroid and sleepless nights,
The fortnightly periods and incessant heavy bleeding
Have not yet proved unbearable.

But even that is nothing
Compared to how
Father's death bed promise
To look after your mother
Whom he died on
Rather than face another day of her cruelty.
Now you feel this debt is being called on again as

Your brother already blind and crippled from diabetes
Is planning his own suicide and escape
To emulate your father,
with his favourite niece,
Your daughter,
Cast as you,
Being bound
To the devil
With the anger, grief and hate
Swelling up inside
Until it turns into a living cancer
Consuming the body tissue.

The Son

I sit and listen.
His father found his soiled underpants.
They were baked solid.
He leaves bottles of urine around.
He stays in bed all day.
He never goes to sleep at night.
He's always playing his record player.
He breaks everything we give him.
He never wears the clothes I buy for him.
I feel he hates us.
No. More dislikes.

(I should have just shut up,
Let it come.)

The son recalls a string of put downs
His parents no longer claim to remember,
Chastising him like a school kid.

(At last)
I was afraid they would hit me.
us hit him—
When did we?

If anything, we spoilt you!

What about the belt,
the time you hit Melvin and me
After we had turned the pillows out
All over our room.

Vague memories.

(I can't quite get hold of the feelings.)
It's not rolling that easy tonight.
There's not enough space in me.)

He gives up all his jobs.
He just goes out in the morning.
Do you know
I used to find his sandwiches,
The ones I had made,
In the fields, on garage roofs.
The jobs paid well
But he just didn't turn up.
He didn't tell us.
We did everything for him.
I take him to the psychiatrist.
I drove him to the dole.
Do you know
He used to go in the door
And still not sign on.
So I had to come right in
And up to the desk with him
And once he altered his benefit cheque.

We do all this for him,
Show him our love
And he spurns us.

It is as if
The relationship with the son
Contains the dark side of the family's feelings.
We treat him no different from any of the others.
No!
He is a disappointment to you.
You can't understand why he throws
Everything back in your face,
Hates you.

How do you feel son about what your parents say?
I agree.
But later, politely,
I love you.
How far back do I have to go
To find the roots?

Depression

It came to me today,
While contemplating relationships
In my household
That one of the characteristics
Of people who are labelled
Mentally ill
Is that they are self-centred
And do not consider where others are at
Or, at least,
As they dump their emotions, *
Do not know,
Or aren't bothered
What effect this might have,
Or,
Are only too well aware of the effect,
But only in so far as it gratifies
Their own needs,
As they watch with pleasure
Others flailing around in their debris.

At work, on the ward,
We set up groups, with power,
So that people are made aware

Of the consequences of their actions.
At home, however,
People say piss off
If you don't like the taste of my garbage
Go eat someone else's;
And if it's their house,
Or their money or job and
You are a bit of their property,
A servant, wife, or tenant,
Carrying out domestic duties,
Without power,
You shut up,
Or at least I do,
Looking forward,
To my next day at work.

Dennis

Dennis lives alone in his flat,
Overlooking the industrial waste of the city,
Amidst the debris of
Rotting food, half-drunk cups of tea,
Grease stained cooker and floor;
Shouting abuse at all
Who dare to come to the door.

All alone his paranoia ran riot,
Hitting out at all who wanted to help.
Mind you we offered too little too late
When he had moved from the hostel,
Stopped coming to the day hospital
And we had all turned away to others,
So by the time we remembered to care
He was a long way down the hill
Watching out for the gestapo
Of the welfare state waiting to entrap him.
And even the hospital social worker said
She was too busy.

His wife had kicked him out
He was told he could no longer see the children.

He was fired from his job.
He had only £3.95 a week for his pleasure;
Not enough after fags to buy his round of drinks.
So he remained alone at home,
Only venturing out now and again
To snarl at those who kicked him
(Nasty ill-tempered bugger they said of him)
And all their agents and abettors.

He turned on his fellow patients.
He turned on us and the social services;
And in the end, he turned
Against the only person left – himself.
And as he deteriorated

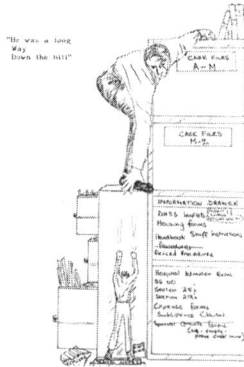

There was little we could do but watch
And warn the main hospital
That they would soon have a readmission.

Alison

Alison found it difficult to believe
That someone might not love her
Not give in to all she wanted.

If flouted she would cry,
Stamp her foot and call mummy
Who would tell her not to be
Such a silly, naughty, child.
Alison, duly chastened
Would apologies, kiss, hug
And say I love you
To anyone who stood close by.

When told it wasn't the done thing
To hug and kiss indiscriminately
She said: why not?

Why not?
Because the innocents are slaughtered.
In social skills we demolish their ideas
And leave them defenceless
With consummate ease.
Mum's love retained its stranglehold

And Alison continues to eat her fill of
Cream buns
And dream of holidays abroad.

Lucky, lucky Alison
To be smothered so.

The Space Poems
1. Your Space or Mine?

Some nights, between one day and the next.
I run out of time and dreams
To sort through the accumulated hassles
So my head can find some space.

Without the space
My head is too crowded
To hear anything
But its own nightmares.

The next day I act therapy.
But there is no healing,
Because as nothing is given
Nothing changes for the better.

That's why I hate you.
You give nothing,
But rotate all day
On your axis
In between scenes
With your lovers
Among the patients

Demanding their devotion,
Threatening rejection,
Abusing your power,
Keeping them waiting
Competing for commissions
To attend to your needs.
Dividing them,
Ruling them,
Despising them
For their dependence.
Too scared to love
In case someone might say no

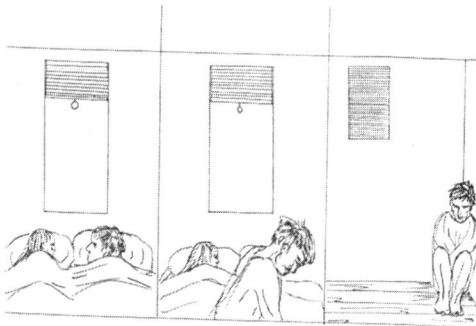

"I run out of time and dreams"

And you would end up alone
With too much time
And nothing to fill your space
But the memories
You try to hide from.
It could also be
I hate you most

On the days
I see in you
Some parts of me
Without the space
To let them be.

2. The Space Inside

Therapy is treating
Clients as friends,
Being open.
Giving them the space*; time**, and energy***
To try out
Their fears and hopes
And explore their tragedies;
Being aware
Of the effect on yourself,
Responding with affection,
Occasional interpretation
And relevant bits of your own history
They can compare with their own.

It is not:
Putting your emotions to one side,
Becoming the mirror
For them to lay
Themselves and their troubles
Out on display
For your clinical head

"I see in you
Some parts of me."

Space is the room left
When your own troubles
Have been put to rest,
To let new thoughts and feelings emerge
And to hear what others are saying.

***

Time is primarily quantitative,
A necessary but not sufficient condition
For other things to take place,
Whose value depends
On what is done with it.
There is no point in having the time
If the space isn't there
Nor the energy to work through things.

***

Energy is the emotional force
Fed by success, recognition and love,
Drained by boredom, lack of control and
Nothingness,
That in differing amounts
We have available for each encounter.
When the energy runs out
The space fades away
And despite the amount of time available
We are too tired to do anything about it
Except long for sleep.

3. The Day Space Ran Out

My head gave out.
I mumbled something,
Staggered upstairs
And collapsed into bed.
When I awoke later
They had gone home
Leaving the house awash
With the debris of dinner.

Enough is enough.
Last week for example
I did the work of 4 people
Owing to staff shortages.

The student on training today
Said the place was more like a family than
A ward.
People talked to each other
And enjoyed themselves.
But it takes a lot out of you
To give the support and love
That makes it happen,
And some days all you get in return

Is abuse and indifference.

In the end
The energy runs out.
I just need a peaceful time,
Then some love and friendship
For the space to return
So, I have something
Again, to offer.

I could struggle in I suppose,
But it would be going through the motions,
Helping management believe
We could continue
But it's my health
That's at risk
And when that goes
I'm not helping anyone
Except the pockets
Of the monetarists.

I'm phoning in sick
What do we put on the form?
Exhaustion!
Just put exhaustion.

4. Surviving

What is the nature?
Of my contract with the state?
They pay me a wager – Minimal as it is
In return they expect me
To contain some
Of my mentally ill friends
And rehabilitate others
To be further exploited
In their productive labour
By bosses and husbands.

They pay for my time
My skills,
But most importantly
For my energy.
In return they expect
A certain level of productivity.
The health authorities
Who visit our day hospital
Are always asking:
How many have you got back to work?
How many have you got attending?
Or to paraphrase it:

How many people
Do we shut up
For each worker we employ?

We are however,
Not merely warders.
We strive to give people
The skills and confidence
To transform their lives
And situations.
But this takes energy
The surplus left over
Once the state has taken its due.

The state would rather
We remain alienated from our work,
That what spare energy there is,
Is dissipated elsewhere,
That we see our members
As mentally ill objects
To be filed and processed
Along agreed channels.

Therefore we have always
To fight our employers
For the right to be committed.
This takes some of our energy.
We need to support our fellow workers
So that there is solidarity.
This takes some of our energy.
We need to build up the union

To protect ourselves.
This takes some of our energy.
With public expenditure cuts
Fewer of us
Are expected to look after more of them.
Therefore more energy is taken
Just to earn your wage
And in the need to resist.
Even less is left to fight
with our patients
Against their oppression.
Therefore we have to take energy
From every available source.

In the end the cracks emerge:
"You're always tired when you come home!"
"You don't give very much at work anymore."
"You've missed the last three union meetings."
In the end
Something has to give.
Which is how,
In part,
In one way or another,
One generation of activists
Becomes
The next generation of sell-outs.

BOB

Why are you always on your own
When you ask everyone to be your friend?

The thing is, you creep about
Pouncing upon people,
Demanding that they love you,
Beseeching them for emotional alms,
Pulling at them to hug you.

But it doesn't work
People shrink and shrivel away,
Freaked by the bottomless pit
Of need you flash at them.

Finally you resort to verbal bombardment
With offers of marriage and love.
To escape, people plead assent
Then hide in corners till you pass.

We started trying to get you
To keep your distance,
Using drama exercises

To show you how people
Were threatened
When you came too close.

But it didn't really work,
Because people like some people more than others;
And it was difficult for you to understand
Why the hand that pushed you away
Would clasp another.

You are addicted to your need.
Little wonder, given that you were:
Abandoned by your parents;
Brought up by a strict auntie who did not spare the rod;
Sent off to a special school
Then children's homes and finally
They put you in a mental hospital.

God – probably no one has ever held you with affection,
Even once.
No wonder you ask so desperately
For what you haven't had, can't get,
And unless we can help,
Never will.

So we must try and meet the need,
Wanted: the ad might read:
A substitute mother
For an unattractive 20-year-old male,
Who will want to grope you
And be cuddled in return.

In need of sexual guidance
(Though you are not expected to provide the practice)
And a lot of emotional warmth.

Any volunteers?

"You creep about pouncing on people"

Mother and Child

Susan asked Alan:
"Why does Brian hug me?
Does he love me more than his wife?"

She started the hugging
He protested, when accused.
Anyway, I was just being friendly.
Anyway look at her life
She needs some affection.
Put in a children's home before she was five
She was transferred to a mental hospital
On her eleventh birthday.
Then after she had fought her way out twelve years later,
They took her child off her.

She's been fighting ever since.
They say she's manipulative,
She terrorises people, she bullies,
She occasionally throws fits to get attention.
Even if sometimes it might be correct
Why don't they also say
She cares.
But they are not taught

To see the oppressed can be good.
It might raise some doubts about how the mad are treated
If the disturbed are recognised as human.
By what right do they have to say to her
"I accuse."

She's been fighting ever since.
Fighting for a house,
For the skills to cope with 'normal' life,
For the child to be returned.
You must remember reader,
Those twenty years of institutionalised life
Is not the best preparation for survival.

But this is life.
They say
we must proceed slowly.
remember how disturbed she was;
remember the child.
she must prove herself some more—

We counsel tact – remember they have power
To keep hold of your child.
You must control this honesty
In openly showing your feelings, your anger.
Normality is about practicing deceit;
Calling enemies, friends;
Smiling while you put the knife in.
This discussion is also called social skills training.
Too much reality is bad for anyone.
Remember it's what they got you for last time.

You couldn't act.

So what they ask is always unreasonable.
Reader, ask yourself, honestly,
Could you keep your temper
When teased by the abductor of your child?
Because if you don't,
If you really express what you feel,
They say:
See – she's blown it,
We were right to go slowly.
She's not ready yet.

Oh Kramer v Kramer did you simplify things.
Our Susan has to win more than an Academy Award
To get custody
With no opportunities for retakes
If she fluffs her lines.
It's all faithfully recorded
Even the number of times she slammed the door.
For them, your future guardians
1984 has already come.

Yes Susan your fighting spirit does attract.
It ain't love, or anything particularly sexual,
Just respect and affection
For a very battle-scarred warrior
With a lot of anger inside her
Who's got a long way to go.

To bring you up to date reader,

At the moment Susan is allowed to see her daughter
For 2 hours every three weeks.
I think they call it,
"maintaining the relationship".
The meeting used to be
At the child's nursery
With the staff popping in
Every ten minutes or so,
Just to see everything was alright.
"Pretend everything is normal."

Poor Susan
Having to act that
She was in a non-existent house
With a child who was already hers
Where invisible intruders did not walk unasked through
The door,
The clock on the wall wasn't rushing the minutes away.

They, the watchers, reported:
"She doesn't seem to know how to hold the child properly;
She looked uneasy when it cried;
She didn't appear to relate to him very well."
It was all faithfully written down.
Then they thought she was unreasonable,
Making unnecessary difficulties
When she said she wanted to see her child
At our place instead of the nursery.

If she lasts out another six weeks
And if the case review then recommends it,

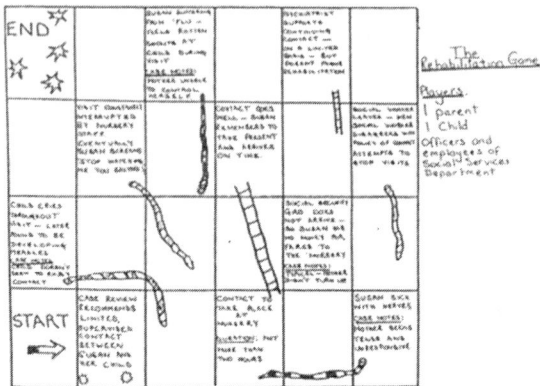

"It's all faithfully recorded" (118)

And if the committee approves the recommendation,
They will begin to work towards her getting her child back;
Not this year mind you, perhaps next.
We can't promise anything,
We must build up the contact slowly,
We can't rush these things.
And all this time
Susan must keep it together
Knowing any outburst
Will be added to her bulging file,
To be remembered
When it can be best used against her.
Could you do it reader?
Could you?
Now you know reader
How they, the concerned
Handle these things

In a caring community.
Doesn't it fill you full of hope
For the time to come
When we all will be caring, concerned people.

The Mindless Tin Drum

I went and saw the Tin Drum
Having sneaked away from a conference,
Entitled 'whither psychiatric day care?'
We were simply non speaking extras
Someone for the papers to be presented to,
Until they could be bound
And submitted to a government minister,
In a blaze of publicity
So everyone would know
What a good job the conference organisers were doing.

The papers were mostly given by researchers,
Living a good life on our sweat
And our patients' problems.
They talked of models, diagnoses, classifications
And semantic differentials.
They didn't mean a thing
Except to the other experts
Who asked intelligent sounding questions
Amidst much backslapping and praise
For each other's contributions.
It was only in the pub at lunchtime
Having sought out like-minded spirits

That the conference made sense.

We talked about pay and conflict, stress and working conditions,

Compromises and deals,

The bread and butter of daily life.

But you can't really expect academics,

Isolated and imprisoned by money, status and good food,

And carrying heads blinded from the arrogance

Of lecturing to students too young to know better,

To be in touch with reality.

Dave
What's It All For?

I was still feeling concussed
So I can't remember very clearly
Everything Dave said.

He was trying to explain
How pointless it was
To start yet another unskilled job
On Friday morning.

Work filled in your days,
But in the evenings you were still alone
With nothing to do but watch television.
Years before he had belonged to a motor-bike gang
But his mates had all got married
And he had nothing left in common with them.
He could see that marriage
Was something that gave you
A purpose to your day
And something new to moan about
With your mates in the evening.
But there was no one he loved;
Without loving there was no caring

124

And without that the purpose would be lost.

It were, he explained, as if life
Was a pointless boredom
In which work, marriage
And the occasional hobby
Filled in the gaping hole
Of nothingness.
Without them he settled for
The minor pleasure of drinks and fags
As hooks to haul himself through the day.

The sense of aimlessness
Had started when his mother died.
If nothing else, families provide
A framework, an enclosed world
In whose labyrinth
An entire universe can be built.
I didn't know what to say.
From the individual's lookout
What purpose could there be
But personal satisfaction.
If you were unlucky enough
To be one of the oppressed
Then the minor pleasures
Were all that were normally
Within your grasp.

There was another answer
Forming in the back of my mind
Based on Dave seeing himself

As a person in a social historical context,
Part of human struggle where he with others
Was locked in an eternal contest
To improve their lot
With those who at present controlled their destiny.

But that meaning
Could only be seen
By those who experienced themselves as oppressed.
That is, by those who had to work;
Who were tied by their family commitments
To stick at their job;
Who therefore had to fight with their fellow workers
For a decent wage and working conditions
If they were to survive.

Dave came back on Friday afternoon.
His new job had lasted an hour.
He had had no need to stick at it.
Because he was free to make that choice
He could not hear the second answer to his question
"What's it all for?"

The Hero

Yesterday Dave was John Wayne,
For most of today he's been David Carradine
Doing the things a man should do.

It was a logical development.
He had worked out that for a man in his position,
Unskilled, unloved and broke
Life had little future.

So why not become someone else
Such as a television hero
And grab some of their glory?
After all they are there
To help us escape from reality
(And sell an unwanted commodity or two)
For a couple of hours.
But for some, in the end,
There is no point in returning.

I last saw him,
Head buried in Dylan.
Getting ready to walk off into the sunset.
Pity it was raining.

More on Dave

Sitting,
Waiting in a freezing bus
For Dave,
No longer big Dave,
Poor scared, frightened Dave
Not nearly so brave,
Neck stiff
Body tense,
In there signing on,
Waiting for a hostel place,
Trouble is they know his face
Remembering too well his past
Know it's likely he won't last
He'll be back inside again
Looney bin or prison pen
Life is always very grave
When you're someone just like Dave
Whom no one knows how to save.

Today at work he couldn't move
Lay on the bed in the same grove.

I undressed him, washed his tummy
All he wanted was a mummy
To cuddle close, to hold him tight
Banish the fears that roam at night.
He staggered off, a walking tree
Finding it hard now he was free
We can't you say befriend them all
Won't tell you then what did befall
Poor Dave in his last hour of need
We'll let him die, we'll let him bleed.

An Ode to Fostering

Crazy little girl,
Alien shapes in an adult world,
Hold you captive,
Play along,
Must get you home soon.

Bye bye Daddy.
Can I stay?
Not now.
Mummy's shadow visits.
The social worker sits in her car.
The foster parents wait.

When will I see you again?
She'll let you know.
In the car
As she goes
Driving you off.
It's for your good
There's nothing I could,
There's nothing I should
They said
At the review,

No preview,
Given to me straight
Man to man.
Best for the child.

Can I stay a little longer?
Not now.
But don't you love me?

In the background stood the law,
One at the gate, one at the door,
Just to make sure nothings amiss
Just to make sure she's had a piss,
It's a long journey
For a little 'un.
Best for her
Given what's happened,
A new life
We'll reconsider if
You find yourself
A new wife,
Respectable
Less strife.

What's the home like?
They're very experienced.
It's what the team leader
Says you always say
When they always ask
Defusing anxiety
By reassurance,

An insurance,
In establishing
Rapport.

Daddy, daddy,
I've hurt myself.
I don't know how
Otherwise to tell you
I hurt inside,
Inside these strangers
Who smile
And bandage my knee
Instead of the pain.

Damn!
I hear the car door slam.
My bandage daddy,
Give me a hug.
I hate you!
Go away!
Don't touch me,
Never,
Ever again.
I'll piss my bed,
Smash my head,
Run into the lane,
Hurt my brains,
Insane, insane,
How else to explain
The scream
Inside my head.

Don't make me go,
Please don't let go
You'll never know,
Hear the silent blow
Of the welcoming smile.
Don't turn away,
It's only been a day.
Send them away.
Keep me another day.
Please.

She sat outside in the car,
Yawned,
Finished her sandwich,
Quarter to nine
Before she'd be home,
John there alone,
Angry.
Looked impatiently at the door.
She had said half past four.
He was late,
Dragging it out,
Time to take her back.
Stroked her head
Wild thought of bed
And the fact that
This was the last trip.
They'd recommend adoption
Child upset after each visit home,
Can't leave her with her dad alone
Fostering must not be short term.

At last research had shown
Child needs to know her place
Recognise her own space.
Thought of John's cock,
Came a little
In her frock.
Got out,
Slammed the door,
Just this once more.

Man cried,
A little bit died.
All done for the best
At society's behest.
Crying's good she said,
Get it off your chest,
Don't stay alone.
As a last resort
Use your phone.
All ends neatly tied,
Time for beddy bies,
She thought,
Looking strangely,
At the child
Sitting silently beside her,
Wonder what's going on in her head

I Had a Dream

I walked to work
With the dream in my hands
That when I told management
I was thinking of leaving
They would be so concerned
At losing someone of my ability
That they would beg me to stay.

Silly me!

I soon awoke.
There were no phone calls,
Just an offer to write a reference.

In the end
I, or any other individual, didn't matter.
All that did
Was that there were 6 staff
Looking after 40 people
So that the books balanced
And the hospital wasn't falling too far behind
Other hospitals falling behind DHSS guidelines,
And papers could be written for area committees

Convincing them
What a good job the authority did.

With so many teachers, social workers
And other graduates out of work
I was easily replaceable
(And with a bit of luck
My successor wouldn't be as militant).
So why waste money
On staff support or training?
If I or others got pissed off and left
It was three months' salary saved
Before the job would be filled.

And every little bit counts these days if there are not to be
compulsory redundancies said the chairman appealing to the
union that he was doing his best in the face of the most vicious
attack on working class living standards since the 1930s.